Sports:

It's All In
the Family

$\mathfrak{Sports:}$

It's All In
the Family

By Marc Catapano

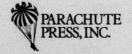

PARACHUTE
PRESS, INC.

Parachute Press, Inc.
156 Fifth Avenue
New York, New York 10010

First Printing: October 1991
Printed in the U.S.A.

Design by Michel Design

COVER PHOTO CREDITS:
Gerald Wilkins: Brian Drake/Sportschrome
Dominique Wilkins: Scott Cunningham
The Ripkens: Focus On Sports
The Hulls: Mark Buckner

CONTENTS

Introduction...7

The Hulls: *Brett Hull, a Star in His Own Right*............9

The Griffeys: *Father and Son Make History* 14

The Millers: *Reggie Steps Out of Cheryl's Shadow* 20

The McGwires: *The Two-Sport Family* 29

The Grants: *Identical Twins Fool the NBA*................35

The Ripkens: *Three Ripkens Are Together Again*........40

The Cunninghams: *Two Brothers Meet the Challenge* 45

The Wilkinses: *The NBA's Dunking Duo* 51

The Bondses: *Baseball's 30/30 Family* 56

The Alomars: *Three Alomars at the All-Star Game*....61

The Davises: *Glenn Finds His Purpose in Life*..........66

The Perrys: *Out of the Fridge's Shadow* 72

INTRODUCTION

Something is going on in the sports world. Ken Griffey, Sr., and Ken Griffey, Jr., hit back-to-back home runs for the Seattle Mariners. Identical twins Horace and Harvey Grant battle it out in the National Basketball Association (NBA). Barry Bonds and Brett Hull remind fans of their famous fathers. And there's Cheryl and Reggie Miller, basketball's All-Star brother and sister. More and more, it seems that when it comes to sports, it's all in the family.

Although there have never been as many sports families competing at once as there are now, history shows that sports families are definitely not a new phenomenon. In baseball during the 1920's and '30's, brothers Paul and Lloyd Waner hit so well for the Pittsburgh Pirates that they both made the Hall of Fame. In 1934, pitchers Paul and Dizzy Dean, another pair of brothers, combined for 49 wins in leading the St. Louis Cardinals to the world championship.

Perhaps the best-known baseball family are the DiMaggios: Vince, Dominic, and Joe. All three of them made the major leagues, and Joe was voted into the Hall of Fame. Although Dominic wasn't quite as great as Joe, he was a fine player, too. When Joe and the Yankees played Dominic's Red Sox team in Boston, fans would taunt Joe by shouting: "Better than his brother Joe, Dominic DiMaggio."

All-time home-run champion Henry Aaron's brother,

Tommie, played major league ball during the 1960's, as did the three Alou brothers: Felipe, Mateo, and Jesus. In fact, in 1963, the Alou brothers played all three outfield positions in a game for the San Francisco Giants.

In football, Doug Flutie threw passes and his brother Darren caught them for the New England Patriots. During the 1960's and '70's, the battles between Oakland's offensive guard, Gene Upshaw, and his brother, Marvin, defensive tackle for the Kansas City Chiefs, were legendary.

Basketball had the Van Arsdale twins, Tom and Dick, whose statistics were as similar as their appearances. In hockey, all-time great Gordie Howe came out of retirement to play with his sons Marty and Mark during the 1970's. And the list goes on. It seems that in sports, as in life, family matters.

THE HULLS: BRETT HULL, A STAR IN HIS OWN RIGHT

The "Great One," Wayne Gretzky, may still be the biggest name in the game, but with the emergence of Brett Hull, he now has company as the National Hockey League's (NHL) symbol of greatness. Brett Hull, son of hockey legend Bobby Hull, is hockey's most exciting rising star.

The past two seasons have been a whirlwind for Brett Hull. After scoring 41 goals for the St. Louis Blues during the 1988–89 season, Brett shocked the hockey world the following year by scoring an outstanding 72 goals. These included 50 in his first 50 games—a truly incredible feat! His father never did this. In fact, only four men in the history of the game had ever done such a thing—Maurice Richard, Wayne Gretzky, Mario Lemieux, and Mike Bossy.

"Being with these four names is something to be proud of," Brett commented. "They all made a name in history. I have a lot of time ahead of me. Maybe I can, too."

Brett took another step forward in history in the 1990–91 season. He again scored 50 goals in 50 games and finished with 86 goals—the second-highest total ever. Brett proved that he's worth the $2 million a year the Blues pay him by winning the Hart trophy, awarded to the NHL's Most Valuable Player (MVP). Brett's selection made NHL history. He and his father thus became the first father-son combination to ever win the NHL MVP award. (Bobby Hull won back-to-back MVP awards in 1965 and 1966.)

Bobby Hull: the Golden Jet

Despite his achievements, Brett still hasn't made fans forget his father. Bobby Hull starred for the Chicago Black Hawks during the 1960's and '70's, and was nicknamed the "Golden Jet." The nickname fit. He had wavy blond hair and was a tremendously fast skater. Many still consider him to be the best ever to play the game.

Bobby played aggressively. His blond hair would fly back as he raced down the ice, ripping through the opponents' defense. If not the best player ever, Bobby was certainly the most exciting. With a shot that traveled more than 100 miles per hour, the Golden Jet scored 610 career goals and finished fourth on the NHL's all-time scoring list.

Bobby and Brett Hull celebrate Brett's 50th goal.

Brett Develops His Own Style

Brett's style of hockey is entirely different from his father's. He waits for the action to come to him. He plays like a ghost—seeming to disappear one minute, then suddenly appearing again with a clear shot at the goal. He doesn't shoot as hard as his father did, but he scores more goals.

"The more I play against Brett," observed New York Ranger goalie Mike Richter, "the more I realize that it's not the heaviness of his shot—a lot of guys have a heavy shot—it's his release."

Brett has his own thoughts on the matter. "My personal philosophy has always been to expend more brain energy than body energy," he said. "To me the game is all fun. When I go out there, I'm having a blast. I guess I'm a goal scorer. I mean, I'm not flashy at all. I make the occasional nice play. I don't do anything that terribly exciting, you know."

Brett's laid-back style of play has helped him to gain his own identity rather than being seen as just Bobby Hull's son. "This way, if anyone said to me, 'You're not as good as your dad,'" Brett explained, "I could say, 'I don't play like him, so how could you compare us?'"

As Brett grew up, he began to play more seriously. Brett constantly reminded himself that he would never play like Bobby Hull, and that all that mattered was being pleased with his own efforts.

"You see, I learned how to be Bobby Hull's kid a long, long time ago," he said.

Brett's Childhood

Being Bobby Hull's son wasn't always easy. When Brett was 14, his parents got divorced. It was a very bitter breakup and was front-page news throughout Canada. Brett moved to Vancouver, British Columbia, with his mother and brothers. He rarely saw his father.

"I'm real close to my mother," explained Brett. "As a kid, I didn't see a lot of my father. We were always distant, but never bitter—we'd talk on the phone, and I'd see him a couple of times a year. He's my dad, and I love him."

Experts think that Brett Hull has just begun to reach his potential. Instead of playing junior hockey like most Canadian players, Brett opted to attend the University of Minnesota at Duluth. After his collegiate playing days were over, Brett joined the Calgary Flames in 1986. St. Louis head coach Brian Sutter said, "You have to realize that Brett didn't play in the NHL for a full season until he was 23. He didn't turn pro when he was 18 or 19, the way Gretzky and some of these other guys did. Everything that's come to him, he's had to grow into." At first he gave the impression that he didn't like to work, but that's not true at all. He just didn't realize how hard he would have to work.

With his good looks and explosive scoring, Brett is seen as the player who will succeed Wayne Gretzky as the NHL's biggest star. However, Brett's coach feels that he still has a way to go, and Brett agrees.

"I'm just a piece of the puzzle here," said Brett. "I'm just a guy who likes to play and have fun. I know that, being the guy who scores the goals and does some clutch things for us, the guys look up to you a little bit. But I'm really not very good at that, not as good as I should be. I'm still learning how to be a good leader. I'm still working at that."

When Brett works that out, the NHL will never be the same.

THE GRIFFEYS: FATHER AND SON MAKE HISTORY

In 1990, Ken Griffey, Sr., and Ken Griffey, Jr., of the Seattle Mariners made baseball history. They became the first father and son to get hits in the same inning and the first father and son to hit back-to-back home runs. In fact, they were the first father-son pair to play in the major leagues at the same time.

Ken Jr., Superstar

Ken Jr. tore up the American League (AL) in 1990. He hit .300, with 22 home runs, and drove in 80 runs. In addition, he swiped 16 bases and played a brilliant center field. Veteran baseball observers raved about his abilities. Many compared him with Hall of Famer Willie Mays. One publication called Ken Jr. the player of the '90's. "People are comparing him with Jose Canseco," said former teammate Matt Young. "He's

14

only 20 years old. Jose was 22 when he made it into the major leagues."

"He's a big kid—a baby," said Gene Clines, the Mariners' hitting coach. "When he finally buckles down and gets serious about this game, there's no telling what kind of numbers he'll put on the board."

Ken Jr. made the Mariners after leading the team in hits and RBI's during the 1989 spring training. At age 19, he was well ahead of schedule in reaching the majors but still batted a solid .264. He finished third in the voting for Rookie of the Year. At the end of the season, though, Ken Jr. got hurt and fell into a slump after returning to the lineup. "He was trying to catch up with the other Rookie of the Year candidates with one swing," said Seattle manager Jim Lefebvre. "Pretty typical for a 19-year-old kid, really. He lost his poise."

"I was worrying about hitting the ball 700 feet," said Griffey. "I just wanted 20 home runs."

Griffey's defense also made people notice him. "Every time he makes one of those plays, you think, he'll never top that one," said Lefebvre. "You can't believe how much it picks up the entire club. He's going to be one of the real marquee players in this league."

"That's why I like playing defense," Ken Jr. said. "It's the only time I get to see somebody else besides me get mad."

Ken Griffey, Jr. and his dad relaxing in the outfield.

Ken Sr.'s Career

Ken Sr. broke in with the Cincinnati Reds in 1973, when Ken Jr. was 3 years old. He made an immediate impression by hitting .384 in 25 games (in 86 at bats). Impressing manager Sparky Anderson, Griffey Sr. was inserted as a full-time starter in 1975 and responded by hitting .305. This helped the Reds win 108 games and defeat the Boston Red Sox in the World Series. The following year, Griffey Sr. was even better. He hit .336, which was only .003 points behind league header Bill Madlock of the Chicago Cubs. The Reds again won the World Series, this time sweeping the New York Yankees.

The Cincinnati Reds of 1975 and 1976 are considered to be one of the greatest teams of all time. Among Ken Sr.'s teammates were Hall of Famers Joe Morgan and Johnny Bench, such All-Stars as Dave Concepcion, Tony Perez, and George Foster, and, at third base, Pete Rose, the all-time major league hits leader. Sometimes Ken Sr. brought young Ken Jr. into the clubhouse to mingle with these legends. Ken Jr. was learning baseball at an early age by watching the best.

"When Ken Jr. was a kid, he wasn't hanging around with just any baseball team," said Seattle catcher, Scott Bradley, who, like the rest of the Mariners, watched Griffey's progress with wonder. "He was hanging around one of the best teams of all time: The Big Red Machine. Pete Rose. Tony Perez. Johnny Bench. So when he comes to the Seattle Mariners, he's supposed to feel like he doesn't belong?"

Mariners Together

Ken Jr. excelled at baseball immediately. He was a star at every level. While still in high school, he began to attract attention from major league scouts. He was drafted first overall in the 1987 amateur baseball draft, right out of high school and ahead of older, college players.

At first Ken Jr. was overconfident about how quickly his career in baseball would take off. "I'll be in the Rookie League for one week, then move to San Bernardino, California [Class A], then Double A the week after that," he told his teammates. "I gotta be in the Show [the majors] when I'm 18, because I have no money left."

"That was when I was young and dumb," said Ken Jr.

While Ken Jr. didn't progress quite as quickly as he thought he would, he did join the Mariners ball club in two years. This made him, at age 19, the youngest player in the game.

As for Ken Griffey, Sr., after nine seasons with the Reds, he joined the New York Yankees. He stayed with the Yankees for five seasons, then went on to play for the Atlanta Braves. Finally, in 1988, Ken Sr. rejoined the Cincinnati Reds, managed by old friend Pete Rose. At age 38, he was back home.

Late in the 1990 season, Ken Sr. was released by Cincinnati. The Mariners quickly picked him up. For the first time, a father and son were playing on the same team at the same time. Ken Sr. hit even better than his son, batting a remarkable .377 in 21 games. Going into the 1991 season, opponents had not only one Griffey to worry about, but two of them.

THE MILLERS: REGGIE STEPS OUT OF CHERYL'S SHADOW

Playing basketball did not always come easy to Reggie Miller. While growing up, Reggie was a very good basketball player. He was tall and had an accurate long-range jump shot. But it was his sister Cheryl who got all the attention. Cheryl was considered the greatest woman basketball player of all time.

One night Reggie scored 39 points for the Riverside Poly High School boys' basketball team only to be overshadowed by his sister, who had scored an incredible 105 points that night for Riverside Poly's girls' team.

"We set a national brother-sister record," bragged Saul Miller, their father. He knew it was important to keep things in perspective.

Growing Up

Cheryl and Reggie Miller grew up in Riverside, California. Cheryl is a year older than Reggie. From an early age, she loved to play basketball. She hung a poster of flashy basketball great Pistol Pete Maravich in her room, and carried a basketball around wherever she went. Their father, a 6-foot-5-inch Air Force computer programmer, encouraged Cheryl to play ball when she was young. Soon Cheryl began playing on the court with Reggie and other boys. Reggie used to challenge his friends to games against him and his sister. "Cheryl would come out of the bushes," he said. *"Boom, boom*—she'd shoot and we'd win. The guys were awed."

Cheryl's older brothers did their best to toughen her up, too. "They made my life miserable," Cheryl said. "They'd trip me, make me skin my knees, and then laugh. They'd constantly remind me that I was adopted [she wasn't]. They'd throw me a ball, tackle me, pile on, mangle me. If I made noise by the TV, they'd make me do push-ups. They'd pay me quarters not to tell Mom and Dad. They wrote me a note: 'You are no longer our sister.' But they were real proud of me for being able to throw and kick balls and fight and stuff. I did everything I could to make them happy. I got so tough I was queen of John Adams grade school."

The Greatest Woman Player in the World

Playing against boys made Cheryl tough. When she began to play organized women's basketball, she continued to use the style she had learned on the playground.

"Cheryl has revolutionized the game," commented women's basketball great Nancy Lieberman. "She has taught young girls to play hard all the time and to be physical. She learned to do that the same way I did— we had to play like the guys."

Some observers felt that Cheryl put on too much of a show when she played. But Nancy Lieberman disagrees. "Her outgoing personality is her bread and butter. She sees those cameras and she seizes the moment. Sure, it's all Hollywood, but that's okay, too. I think Cheryl is the best thing that could have happened to the game."

Cheryl led her University of Southern California (USC) women's basketball team to two collegiate titles. She then went on to star on the U.S. women's team which won this country's first gold medal at the 1984 L. A. Olympic Games. Cheryl's competitiveness and desire to win are what set her apart.

"Just because we're women doesn't mean we don't work or struggle or compete or want to win any less than men," Cheryl said. "I always feel as if I'm a gunfighter and everyone is after me. We can be friends later. On the court, I'm going to take you to the hole and stuff your mug. I'm thinking nothing but net at my end and you'll be lucky to get a shot off me at yours. I'll be in your mug all night—and if you can be intimidated, I'll take advantage of that, too."

Reggie Gets Tough

Basketball did not come quite as easily for Reggie as it did for his sister. When he was young, he had trouble keeping up with Cheryl. Eventually he developed a new weapon in his games against her—size.

"I woke Reggie one day and asked if he was ready for another butt-kicking," Cheryl said. "When he got up, he kept getting up. And up and up. All of a sudden, he was 6 feet 6 inches tall. We went outside for our usual head-to-head game. I took first outs, blew by him like always, and sailed in for the lay-up. As I was running under the basket, I heard this noise. *Clang*. I looked up, and the ball was still up there. So was Reggie. He had pinned it. I stopped in my tracks. 'Uh, Red,' I said, 'how about a game of H-O-R-S-E?'" [Horse is a basketball game in which you try to shoot exactly like the person before you. If you miss, you get an *h*. The first one to get all the letters in *horse* loses.]

After high school, Reggie enrolled at UCLA , USC's crosstown rival. He had trouble as a freshman and averaged only 6 points per game. That's when Reggie began to hear the comments that he was only the second-best player in the Miller family. These comments upset the Miller family.

Reggie Miller taking a breather.

"After that, we called a family meeting," Saul Miller said, "because Reggie was so upset and so were we. Cheryl was here. Darrell [Reggie and Cheryl's older brother and a former major-league baseball player with the California Angels] came. Darrell's the enforcer. We reminded Reggie that whatever Cheryl has become, he helped her get that way. We closed ranks. We also told him to start hitting the boards. From then on, he played like a gangbuster. See, we believe Reggie made Cheryl and Cheryl made Reggie."

After that, Reggie responded by averaging over 20 points per game during his final three years at UCLA. He finished second in all-time scoring with 2,095 points, behind Kareem Abdul Jabbar. This led to the Indiana Pacers making Reggie their first choice in the 1987 NBA draft.

As he had at UCLA, Reggie began to make steady progress—this time for the Pacers. At first he was pushed around by the big pros. They made it hard for him to get off the types of shots he had gotten at UCLA. But by the end of his rookie season he had made progress, finishing with a respectable 10 points per game.

During the 1989–90 season, Reggie came into his own by averaging 24.6 points per game. He also made the All-Star team. He displayed an amazingly accurate long-range jump shot and was moved to guard. Here his height gave him an advantage over his opponents. Reggie was almost as good during the 1990–91 season. He scored 22.6 points per game and established himself as one of the best guards in the league.

Cheryl After Basketball

While Reggie was establishing himself in the NBA, however, Cheryl was facing a dilemma. Her amazing career at USC was over. There was no women's professional league for her to join, and despite her incredible talent, she just wasn't big or strong enough to play in the NBA.

"Much as I love my brother Reggie," she said, "he'll tell me he just signed for X dollars, and I'll think of all the times I just used to stomp him when we were

All-American hero Cheryl Miller.

Dan Helms/Duomo

growing up. I'm not taking any shots at my brother, because he's a fantastic athlete. But for me to go out and do something that I'm very good at and that I really enjoy, I'd have to go overseas."

Cheryl didn't go overseas. She decided to work as an assistant coach at USC. She stayed in shape, planning on trying out for the 1988 women's Olympic basketball team. But one day she suffered a terrible knee injury while playing against some USC football players.

Cheryl recovered enough from her injury to try out for the Olympic team. Her knee just wasn't the same, however, so she decided to pull out of the trials. If she couldn't play like Cheryl Miller, she wouldn't play at all.

Since then, Cheryl has become a sports reporter for ABC Sports. "I've been very fortunate," she said. "I really think broadcasting's my calling. But I don't think anything could actually take the place of playing. I'm a competitor, and I always will be." Nonetheless, Cheryl has ruled out the possibility of becoming a college coach. "I'm a great assistant coach, and I'd like to leave it at that," she said. "I have no desire to become a full-time coach. I don't have the patience. There's too much of the player in me."

Cheryl Miller can be proud of what she has accomplished as a player. She dominated women's basketball as no one before her has ever done. No other woman has yet matched her style and flair for the game. She finished her stellar 4-year career with an average of 23.6 points per game. She was also a 4-time unanimous

All-American selection. Cheryl may not play competitively again, but she can proudly watch her brother score point after point for the Indiana Pacers.

THE McGWIRES: THE TWO-SPORT FAMILY

For Mark and Dan McGwire, 1990 was a big season. Mark hit 39 home runs while helping the Oakland A's capture their third consecutive AL championship. Meanwhile, kid brother Dan had impressed the college football world with his great passing ability as quarterback for San Diego State.

Growing Up

Mark and Dan McGwire, along with their three brothers, grew up in Pomona, California. Their mom and dad were "the best parents in the world," according to Mark. Their father, a dentist, coached Little League and wouldn't leave the park until all of his players had been picked up. Their mother spent much of her time doing community work. While in Pomona, the McGwires grew up . . . *way* up. Mark is 6 feet 5 inches tall and weighs 225 pounds. But he still has to look up to baby brother Dan, who is 6 feet 8 inches tall and weighs 240 pounds.

At one point in high school, Mark actually gave up baseball for golf. But that didn't last longer than one season. The next season he returned to baseball and attracted the attention of the Montreal Expos. They drafted him but, instead of joining the team, Mark decided to attend USC on a baseball scholarship.

When Mark joined USC as a pitcher, he threw hard. His fastball traveled almost 90 miles an hour, and he compiled a 4 wins–4 losses record with a 3.04 earned run average (ERA).

"I had seen him hit in high school and in practice," USC baseball coach Rod Dedeaux said. "I couldn't see wasting him on the mound."

Mitchell B. Reibel/Sportschrome

Mark McGwire smacks another home run.

Mark Makes His Mark

As a first baseman, Mark tore up his college conference
the Pac 10. USC had seen many great players in its
history, including Hall of Famer Tom Seaver and All-
Star slugger Dave Kingman, who hit 404 home runs in
the majors. But none of the others had careers that were
as good as Mark's. As a sophomore, he broke the
record for home runs in one season by hitting 19. The
next year he hit an amazing 32 homers, which is more
than any USC player had ever hit in an entire *career*. In
1985, he was drafted again—this time by the Oakland
A's. Within two years, he had reached the majors. That
was 1987.

Mark had an incredible 1987 season. He led the
majors in home runs, scoring 49. The old record for a
rookie had been 38 homers. Mark was the unanimous
choice for Rookie of the Year.

"He's not your classic power hitter," said the former
Oakland A's hitting coach Bob Watson, "because he
doesn't just pull. He drives the ball from foul pole to
foul pole." Mark's power became the talk of the
baseball world. Mark's strength carries over into golf as
well. He has been known to hit a golf ball 350 yards.

Although he hasn't repeated the success of his rookie
season, Mark has hit more than 30 homers every year
since. No other major league player has ever done that.
Together with teammate Jose Canseco, they make up the
Oakland A's "bash brothers," powering the A's to three
straight World Series.

Dan Impresses the Pros

Danny McGwire stuck to football while in high school. He decided to attend the University of Iowa, where they wanted him to start at quarterback as a freshman.

"After my freshman year in the spring," Dan said, "I earned the right to be the starting quarterback at Iowa. They named me Number One."

He was under the impression that he would have the quarterback job all to himself. But by the next fall, the situation had changed. There were two other quarterbacks competing for the position. Dan was so disappointed he transferred to San Diego State.

Dan's biggest day as a collegian came on December 24, 1990, when San Diego State met Brigham Young University (BYU) at Provo, Utah, and its quarterback, Heisman Trophy winner Ty Detmer. Detmer was brilliant, leading BYU to a 62-34 victory. But Dan's performance was no less impressive. He completed 32 of 59 passes for 362 yards and 3 touchdowns.

"Dan works very, very hard at the game. He listens and takes directions, and that's what's neat about him. Danny can still be much better. His future is ahead of him." San Diego State head coach Al Luginbill said this after Dan had completed his first full-time season of major college football.

"I made a lot of right decisions," Dan said. "I didn't force balls. I threw away balls on purpose. I avoided eight sacks, and I got sacked twice. One was my fault—not the offensive line's fault. My mobility is improving.

Dan McGwire shows off his rifle arm.

I threw for a lot of yards last year and they talked about my strong arm."

After the 1990 season, Dan McGwire was the first quarterback to be chosen by the Seattle Seahawks in the National Football League (NFL) draft. He accomplished this on the strength of some impressive numbers. During his fine collegiate career he passed for 8,164 yards on 575 completions out of 973 attempts, and 49 touchdown strikes. He was overjoyed. By coincidence, the McGwires have relatives and friends in Seattle. Many of them were there when the draft was held. Surrounded by family and friends, Dan used this special occasion to ask his girlfriend to marry him.

Both Mark and Dan are very laid-back and live a California type of life-style. Dan wears polo shirts and shorts to class. He doesn't show off or make a big deal about football on campus. He leads a quiet life.

Reggie Jackson once saw him hit a home run. "It was a bleeping rocket," Jackson said. "I told him he has to stand and watch those home runs." But Mark doesn't like to showboat on the field. "It's not my style," he said.

Because of his mellow attitude, some people think Mark doesn't enjoy playing baseball.

"I have a natural frown on my face," Mark said. "But, actually, I'm happy every day I wake up—excited. It's almost like I'm a kid again out on the field." In their quiet way, Mark and Dan McGwire are two of the biggest stars in sports.

THE GRANTS: IDENTICAL TWINS FOOL THE NBA

Last winter *Sports Illustrated* conducted a poll of NBA coaches to find out which Grant brother people felt was a better basketball player—Horace or Harvey. Denver coach Paul Westhead was a little confused. "Let me get this straight," said Westhead. "Horace plays for the Bullets, Harvey for the Bulls, right?"

Coach Westhead got it right, but he couldn't be blamed for not being sure. No two players in the NBA are so similar. That's because Harvey and Horace are not only brothers but identical twins. There *are* ways to tell the Grants apart. Horace is 6 feet 10, two inches taller than Harvey. Also, Horace is about 10 pounds heavier than Harvey. To make matters easier, Horace wears goggles for protection against eye injury. Harvey does not.

35

Horace Grant at the foul line.

The Grants' Careers

The Grant brothers were born in Augusta, Georgia, on the Fourth of July, 1965. Their careers have followed similar paths. They were both basketball stars at Hancock Central High School in Sparta, Georgia, and were heavily recruited by major colleges. They both decided to attend Clemson University.

Horace played at Clemson for four years, scorching opponents for 21.0 points a game during his senior season. Harvey played at Clemson for only one season, then transferred to Independence Junior College in Kansas. He stayed at Independence for a year before ending up as First Team Junior College All-American at the University of Oklahoma.

Harvey thrived at Oklahoma. Coach Billy Tubbs stressed a wide-open offensive attack, with Harvey at the center of the action. Harvey scored 20.9 points a game during his senior year, leading Oklahoma to an appearance in the NCAA championship game. Unfortunately, they were upset by Danny Manning and the University of Kansas.

Both brothers were drafted in the first round— Horace by the Bulls in 1987; Harvey by the Bullets a year later. Horace immediately played regularly for the Bulls at power forward. He did the dirty work under the boards while Michael Jordan performed his nightly miracles. Horace can score when he gets the chance. He is a very good shooter with an excellent .516 lifetime shooting percentage.

It took Harvey longer to adjust to the NBA. He wasn't quite big enough to play the type of game he had played in college, and he had to learn a new position— small forward. However, during the 1990–91 season, forward John Williams suffered a knee injury and Harvey took his place in the starting lineup. Since he joined the league, Harvey's statistics have improved. His average has jumped nearly 10 points to over 18 points a game, and his shooting percentages have increased to over 50 percent from the floor and 74 percent from the foul line. He has performed superbly, averaging 18.2 points and over 8 rebounds a game.

Harvey Grant—about to make his name.

Al Tielemans/Duomo

Grant Versus Grant

The Grants have met 11 times in their pro careers, with Horace holding a slight statistical edge. When they played each other during Harvey's rookie season, they had fun switching uniforms for warm-ups.

"It took a while for people to figure it out, but they finally did," said Harvey. "We don't do that anymore."

The similarities of their play impress Horace and Harvey Grant themselves.

"It's scary sometimes," said Harvey. "He [Horace] runs exactly the same way I run. I don't know about him, but I'll never get used to playing against someone who looks like me, thinks like me, and is a virtual clone of me."

THE RIPKENS: THREE RIPKENS ARE TOGETHER AGAIN

During the 1987 spring training, the Ripken family was the talk of the baseball world. Cal Jr. was an All-Star shortstop. Younger brother Billy was a hot prospect at second base. And they were managed by their father, Cal Sr., who was being given his chance after 19 years as Baltimore's third-base coach.

Cal Sr. Becomes Manager

Cal Sr. was all baseball. "You talk about outside interests," said one Oriole official, "but I'm not sure Cal has many. He gardens some during the summer and works around the house, but nothing is as important to him as this game. I don't think he'll ever be anything but the last one to leave the field."

Then things began to go wrong. Baltimore lost 95 games in 1987, and when they lost their first six games in 1988, Cal Sr. was let go. Billy and Cal Jr. stayed, however, keeping the Orioles strong up the middle.

The Ripken family—Billy, Cal Sr., and Cal Jr.—relaxing before a game.

The Ripken Household

The Ripken family was a baseball household. Most of the time their father was on the road playing or coaching baseball. Although Cal Sr. didn't push his sons into baseball, they fell into it all the same. He had very little to do with Cal Jr.'s baseball career.

"I didn't get to see too many of Cal Jr.'s games in Little League," Cal Sr. recalled. "So their mother taught him to hit. She was a pretty good hitter herself, and I'm not talking about fanning the kids' behinds." Cal Sr. didn't make a big deal about his job. He thought of baseball as just the thing he did for a living.

"When Dad first asked if I wanted to go to the ballpark with him," said Cal Jr., "I went because I could be alone with him on the drive there and back. Eventually I began to enjoy baseball."

According to Billy Ripken, he and Cal Jr. grew up wearing baseball uniforms. "Even when I was around the big guys," he said, "the natural thing to do was to put on a batboy uniform. That's what I did for my dad's team in Asheville, North Carolina, back in 1972–74. That's what I always assumed I would do."

Eventually the Ripkens moved back to their hometown of Aberdeen, Maryland. Both Billy and Cal Jr. went to Aberdeen High School and were drafted by the Orioles right out of high school.

Cal Jr. and Billy Join Their Dad

In 1982, Baltimore Orioles manager Earl Weaver named Cal Ripken, Jr., his starting third baseman. Cal responded by hitting 28 home runs and winning the Rookie of the Year award. The next year Weaver surprised the baseball world by putting Cal Jr. at shortstop. Cal Jr. is 6 feet 4 inches tall, and nobody that tall had ever played this position before. No one believed a player of that size had the speed needed to scoop up ground balls.

"Cal Ripken, Jr., will be a household name before long," predicted left fielder John Lowenstein. Veteran pitcher Jim Palmer agreed. "He's the best athlete on the team," said Jim, "and I should know because that used to be me."

"Just because Cal Jr. is my son doesn't make him special," insists Cal Sr. "He's one of 25 players on this team, and I'm proud of all these guys. They're all like sons to me." When Cal Sr. was asked what the best thing about having his son on the Orioles was, he answered: Having a shortstop who hits .318.

Cal Jr. was more excited. "Ever since I was a kid," he said, "my dream was to play in the Series. But having my father here to share it with me makes it extra special."

Ever since his rookie season, Cal Jr. has been measured against some of the greatest infielders of all time. Entering the 1991 season he had played 1,476 straight games—second best of all time. In fact, Cal Jr.

didn't miss a single inning between 1983 and 1989. Cal Jr. has hit over 20 home runs each year he's been in the league. Last year he compiled an unbelievable .996 fielding average. It seems likely that when he retires he'll join fellow Oriole greats Jim Palmer, Brooks Robinson, and Frank Robinson in the Hall of Fame.

Unlike Cal Jr., Billy Ripken did not become a star immediately. Though he fielded brilliantly at second base, he had some problems with the bat. He continued to work hard, however, and managed to bat an excellent .291 in 1990. This made him one of the keystones of the team.

"I just want to make it up here," the 6-foot, 1-inch, 180-pound Billy said. "I really believe it's easy to stay if you make that first step. I've been hurt so much I never thought I'd get that one chance."

After losing his job as manager of the Orioles, Cal Sr. kept in touch with the team and up-to-date with manager Frank Robinson's performance. In 1989, Cal Sr. rejoined the Orioles as a coach. He encouraged the players to play hard for Robinson. They responded, helping the Orioles to a remarkable 88 wins in 1989. Cal Sr. has rejoined his sons at Baltimore. Opponents had better watch out. Three Ripkens are better than two.

THE CUNNINGHAMS: TWO BROTHERS MEET THE CHALLENGE

Randall Cunningham is the most talented quarterback in the NFL. He throws the ball like a cannon, leads the Eagles in running with the football, and occasionally even kicks a booming punt. Randall is the younger brother of former USC and New England Patriots fullback Sam "Bam" Cunningham. Although they are years apart in age and play different positions, both Sam and Randall know how to play when the pressure is on.

Randall's Big Game

Randall established himself as a top-line NFL quarterback during the 1989 season. When the Eagles' management rewarded Randall with a multi-million-dollar extension to his contract it immediately paid off.

On the same day he signed the extension, Randall rallied the team from a 20-0 deficit against the Washington Redskins to a 42-37 victory. He fired 5 touchdown passes and completed 34 of 46 passes for 447 yards. "Randall is a talent—a great, natural athlete and a great leader on the field," former coach Buddy Ryan said. "He's made himself what he is. Randall's teammates believe he can do anything." He probably can.

"Last year Buddy came up to me and said, 'It's your offense. If it doesn't work, it's going to be your fault,'" said Randall, looking serious. "I don't mind that at all. Let the pressure be on me—not Buddy. Buddy has given me a home."

Randall Cunningham directs the action.

Sam "Bam"

January 1, 1973. The undefeated USC Trojans met the Ohio State Buckeyes at the Rose Bowl in Pasadena, California. The Trojans were one of the greatest college teams ever, with such future pros as Lynn Swann, Charles Phillips, Pat Haden, and Charles Young. Also on the team was Randall's older brother, Sam.

Sam was nicknamed "Bam" for his hard hitting. He was a fullback whose job was to block for halfback Anthony Davis. But on this day, coach John McKay gave the ball to Sam. Sam "bammed" through the Ohio State defense for 4 touchdowns, leading the Trojans to a 42-17 victory, and was named the Rose Bowl Most Valuable Player.

Sam "Bam" Cunningham was a devastating fullback. Although he was an excellent runner, he was known for his crushing blocks. He started three years at USC. According to the late University of Alabama head coach Bear Bryant, Sam helped make it possible for all races to play for the Alabama football team. Alabama learned its lesson after he scored 2 touchdowns and rushed for 135 yards against an all-white Alabama football team in 1970.

Sam played for the New England Patriots for eight years. During that time, he powered his way to 5,453 yards rushing—a club record. He retired in 1982 and became the owner of a landscaping company.

Sam Cunningham resting on the sidelines.

Randall Reaches His Potential

Randall is 12 years younger than Sam and never got to be very close to him. They both grew up in Santa Barbara, California, and attended Santa Barbara High School. Randall lived in a house that Sam purchased for the family after signing a pro contract.

In football, Randall followed Sam's footsteps, but the Cunninghams kept their priorities in life.

"We all played football," said Randall, "but we all studied, too. If you didn't study, you didn't play."

Although running was one of his greatest strengths, Randall wanted to play quarterback. So he decided against attending USC as Sam had. Instead, he went to the University of Nevada at Las Vegas (UNLV). There he set an NCAA record by being one of only three quarterbacks to pass for over 2,500 yards in three consecutive seasons.

At UNLV (1981–85), Randall compiled some eye-popping statistics. He threw for 8,290 yards, 60 touchdowns, and completed over 57 percent of his passes. In addition to his fine passing skills, Randall excelled as a punter and was named First Team All-American at that position.

"He's a Doug Williams with a touch," said a scout, referring to the former NFL quarterback who is famed for his strong arm. "He can throw any kind of pass you can name. The key thing is that he doesn't throw interceptions. If the draft were held tomorrow, he'd be the first quarterback taken."

"Some people have to strain to learn this game," said UNLV coach Harvey Hyde. "Randall does everything with ease. Just watch him play the game. Football is a very easy game for him to play."

Randall didn't miss a beat in the NFL. He started for the Eagles halfway through his second year (1986), passing for 1,391 yards and 8 touchdowns. Even more impressive, he ran for 540 yards with an incredible 8.2-yard average per attempt. He is the only NFL quarterback, along with Miami's Dan Marino, to start every game since the 1987 strike season.

The next year Randall was even better, throwing for 23 touchdowns and leading the team in rushing. Critics thought he ran too often, but Buddy Ryan disagreed. He believed in Randall and was not disappointed. The Eagles won their division in 1988 and finished second in 1989. Randall passed for over 3,000 yards and led the team in rushing both years. In addition to that, in 1989 Randall again showed his all-around ability by shocking the New York Giants. Randall boomed an amazing 91-yard punt—an Eagle team record.

In 1990, the Eagles again made the play-offs only to lose to the Washington Redskins, who were in turn defeated by the eventual Super Bowl champions, the New York Giants. Buddy Ryan decided to bench Randall for one series. What a mistake that was! It caused such an uproar that Ryan was fired.

Randall felt bad about Coach Ryan being fired. He knew he could have played better. Still, fans know the Eagles would have gone nowhere without Randall in the first place. Randall Cunningham continues to be football's ultimate weapon.

THE WILKINSES: THE NBA'S DUNKING DUO

The 1990 All-Star game in Miami. Some of the greatest athletes in the world assembled for the slam-dunk contest. Kenny Walker, the 1989 champion of the New York Knicks, was there, along with such stars as Seattle's Shawn Kemp and Charlotte's Rex Chapman. But despite the flights of these young legs, the final prize went to 29-year-old 6-time All-Star Dominique Wilkins. Dominique threw down a series of dunks that stunned the judges. Dominique won his second slam-dunk contest, again proving himself king of the NBA's slam-dunk competition.

Gerald Wilkins guards his older brother Dominique.

The Human Highlight Film

By the time Dominique was in his junior year at the University of Georgia, he had gained a national reputation for his skill as a basketball player. His awesome dunking ability was especially outstanding. Standing still, Dominique can jump 47 inches into the air—almost 4 feet! With his size (6 feet 8 inches), jumping ability, coordination, and sense of style, Dominique has accumulated so many amazing dunks that he became known as the human highlight film.

Georgia coach Hugh Durham remembered one example of Dominique's talent: "It was in practice and we were working on breaking the press. One of our guards threw the ball from mid-court sort of wildly toward the basket, toward Dominique, who was standing outside the lane.

"Now, the ball looked like it was going out of bounds. It would've been a real nice play just to catch that ball and keep it in play. But what Dominique did was catch the ball with one hand and slam it down into the basket—in one motion! Heckfire, can you imagine that?

"What happened next was strange. Everything got real quiet on the court for maybe a second or two. Nobody could believe what they'd seen. I still don't believe it."

Dominique was truly "top dawg" for the Georgia Bulldogs. He scored 1,588 points and grabbed 588 rebounds in an abbreviated 3-year career.

Everyone seems to have stories about Dominique Wilkins. "I've got about 30 Dominique stories," said University of Georgia teammate guard Derrick Floyd, "but here's the one that sticks out in my mind: Dominique is coming down the left-hand side and a guard's on him pretty close. It looks like he's going to take a left-handed lay-up, but the guard comes across to get the ball. So what he does is cuff the ball [tuck it into a protective position by rolling it up his wrist], turn his body to cut the guy off, and dunk it backward. It wasn't really a hot-dog play. It was the only thing he could do. But no one else could have done it."

While Dominique was growing up, basketball wasn't his only sport. He was a great marbles player, too.

"I was the Larry Bird of marbles," said Dominique.

"He was one of the best ever," agreed his younger brother Gerald.

When Gerald and Dominique were young, their father left home. The rest of the family stuck together, though, and Dominique assumed much of the responsibilities his father had left behind. Since then, Dominique has forgiven his father.

"I still love him," he said. "Everybody makes mistakes in life."

Dominique wasted little time in making his presence felt in the NBA. As a rookie with the Atlanta Hawks, Dominique averaged over 17.5 points a game and was named to the All-Rookie Team. Each year, he improved until he led the league in scoring with an average of 30.3 points per game in 1987.

Impressive Gerald

Gerald went to the University of Tennessee–Chattanooga, a small school out of the limelight. Despite averaging over 20 points per game, Gerald didn't attract much attention. But he ignored critics' comments that he wasn't as good as Dominique. Through sheer willpower, however, Gerald persevered until he impressed the New York Knicks enough for them to make him their second-round draft choice in 1986.

After Gerald struggled for two seasons, coach Rick Pitino got him more involved in the Knicks' all-around game plan in 1988–89. Gerald responded beautifully. Along with Patrick Ewing and Charles Oakley, Gerald led the Knickerbockers to the Atlantic Division crown. Gerald has improved every year he's been in the league. He has averaged over 15 points per game during his career. He has also impressed observers with his arsenal of dunks. Dominique had better watch out—Gerald is catching up.

THE BONDSES: BASEBALL'S 30/30 FAMILY

In September of 1990, Barry Bonds made history when he became the first Pittsburgh Pirate to hit 30 home runs and steal 30 bases in one season. In fact, he stole 50 bases and became baseball's first 30/50 man. This combination of power and speed is something the major leagues haven't seen since the early 1970's, when a right fielder named Bobby Bonds, Barry's father, reached a 30/30 record five times.

Bobby Bonds and family—1970's style. The one on the left is Barry.

Like Father, Like Son

It's unusual for father-son combinations to resemble each other as much as Barry and Bobby do. Both men are lean batters with quick wrists. Both combine power and speed in a fluid graceful style. Barry bats left-handed and doesn't have quite the strong arm his father has, but he strikes out less. Still, a knowledgeable baseball fan might rub his eyes and be startled by the similarities.

Bobby helps Barry whenever he can. "Whenever we talk on the phone," said Bobby Bonds, "Barry knows I've been there. I've stood 60 feet 6 inches from [Hall of Famers] Bob Gibson and Don Drysdale. There's no situation that comes up for Barry that I haven't gone through myself at one time. The hitting aspect. The mental aspect. Any aspect."

After Barry Bonds won the National League (NL) Most Valuable Player (MVP) award in 1990, it made it a little easier for his father to cope with not having won the award back in 1973.

"The *Sporting News* named me its player of the year," said Bobby. "They gave me a big plaque, but I never put it up in the house. I don't even know where it is now. I wanted the MVP plaque that I thought I deserved."

Bobby Bonds remains Barry's biggest fan. "When Barry came up to the Pirates in 1986 and I was coaching at Cleveland," he said, "the Indians asked me if I wanted to be activated late in the season. I thought about it, but I decided against it. Looking back, I'm kind of glad we didn't play at the same time. There's enough comparisons as it is. I had my time. This is Barry's time."

Bobby Bonds's time was in 1968, when he joined the San Francisco Giants. Bobby played right field alongside the legendary Willie Mays, regarded as the finest outfielder of all times. Willie was winding down a tremendous career that included the major-league record of two 30/30 seasons. Never before had the major leagues seen such a combination of power and speed until the emergence of Bobby Bonds, who hit 30/30 in 1969 and repeated the feat four more times.

"No one gives my dad credit for what he did, and

they want to put me in the same category," Barry said. "He did 30/30 five times, and they say he never became the ballplayer he should have become. Nobody else had done 30/30 five times. Nobody. Zero. So I don't care whether they like me or not."

"What is potential?" Bobby asked. "Why do I have to live up to anybody's expectations? If you use that word, then nobody in this world has been a success, because he has failed somebody's expectations."

Barry Measures Up to Expectations

In 1989, after three outstanding seasons, things became difficult for Barry Bonds. He hit only .248 and the Pittsburgh fans began to get impatient. But under the tutelage of manager Jim Leyland, Barry responded with a monster year. In 1990, with the help of his friend Bobby Bonilla, Barry powered the Pirates to their first NL East Championship since 1979.

Barry works very hard at baseball. He's always trying to make himself a better player. "We'd start working out at 10:30 in the morning," said strength-and-conditioning coach Warren Sipp. "And every day Barry would be in the parking lot, waiting for me."

"Everyone knows I want to be good—very good," Barry said. "I had it figured out that I was going to get a hit in every single game. And when I didn't get a hit the second game of the season, I was mad the whole week.

The whole week. I was mad because I blew my streak. Can you believe that?"

"Barry goes through times when all he wants to do is hit home runs," said one Pirate. "Someone on the other team will go out of the yard, and Barry will try to show that he can do it, too."

Barry thinks back to when he was a kid. "Since I was a kid, I've had a stamp on my neck," he said. " 'Barry Bonds has a bad attitude and only thinks of himself.' Who else am I supposed to think about out there? I go out there to put up the best numbers to help us win. That's being part of the team. Barry Bonds plays hard, he plays hurt, and he goes to the post."

Like his father, Barry has been involved in controversy over pay and attitude. During spring training, Barry got into a heated shouting match with manager Jim Leyland. This incident seemed to bring to a head Barry's anger over his future with the Pirates. Leyland and Barry quickly made up, and Barry apologized to his teammates. Now, Jim Leyland is in Barry's corner again.

THE ALOMARS: THREE ALOMARS AT THE ALL-STAR GAME

During the late 1980's, it looked as if the Alomars would join the Ripkens as baseball's biggest family. Sandy was coaching for the San Diego Padres, and both of his sons had also joined the team. First Roberto came up as a second baseman in 1988. Then catcher Sandy Jr. joined a year later. But in 1989, Sandy Jr. was traded to Cleveland, and soon after, Roberto was traded to Toronto. That left Sandy alone in San Diego.

Sandy Jr., Sandy, and Roberto Alomar—baseball's All-Star family.

Growing Up with Baseball

Sandy Jr. and and his younger brother Roberto grew up in Salinas, Puerto Rico. Since their father was a baseball player for seven different teams, they spent their summers in Chicago, New York, and Los Angeles. Roberto and Sandy were able to go to as many games as they wanted to watch the pros play.

Roberto wanted to know everything about baseball. He studied, analyzed, and worked on each part of his game. The game came more naturally to Sandy Jr. He spent his time at home resting or watching television rather than practicing baseball. Roberto always grabbed the bats or gloves that their father brought home. Sandy Jr. let him.

Sandy's Career

Like his sons, Sandy Alomar was born in Salinas. He was raised there, too. He played in the major leagues for 15 seasons, starting with the old Milwaukee Braves (before they moved to Atlanta). But his best seasons were spent playing second base for the California Angels between 1969 and 1974.

Sandy was a quick, sure-handed fielder who not only played second base but could fill in at almost every position. His value was increased because he was a switch hitter, which meant that he always had an advantage over the pitcher. Because of this versatility and because he was so durable, Sandy broke the all-time AL record in 1971 when he recorded 689 at bats.

Sandy was traded to the Yankees in 1974 and helped them to their best showing in 10 years. In 1976, the Yankees won the AL pennant. Sandy played a key role off the bench, playing every position but catcher and pitcher. After the 1976 World Series, Sandy was traded to Texas, where he finished his career.

Sandy Jr.'s Career

Sandy Jr. (Santos Velazquez Alomar) tore up the minor leagues while playing for Las Vegas, San Diego's AAA (the highest level of the minor leagues) affiliate. In 1988, he hit .297 with 16 home runs, and was named the Minor League Player of the Year by *Baseball America*. After a year like that, a player is usually called up to the major leagues. But the Padres had All-Star Benito Santiago as catcher, so Sandy Jr. remained at Las Vegas. This time around he did even better. He hit .306 and drove in 101 runs. Sandy was again named Minor League Player of the Year.

Because Benito Santiago continued to play so well, the Padres had to do something with Sandy Jr. During the off-season, therefore, Sandy and two other players were traded to the Cleveland Indians.

"I've been in baseball for 29 years," said one Indians coach. "Sandy Alomar is the best catching prospect I've seen since [Hall of Famer] Johnny Bench."

Roberto Adjusts Quickly

Roberto was only 20 years old during his rookie season in 1988, but he played like a veteran. He hit a solid .266, showed speed by stealing 24 bases, and played a beautiful second base. Roberto continued to improve, and in 1989 he upped his average to .295 and stolen bases to 42.

If Roberto was upset with all the attention Sandy Jr. was getting, he didn't show it on the field. He acted extremely mature for such a young player. He became the glue of the Padre infield, participating in 73 double plays in 1990. He again put in an impressive effort, hitting .287, with 24 stolen bases in 147 games.

Although they enjoyed being together on the Padres, the Alomars don't mind going their own ways. "I had two feelings when the trade was made," Sandy Jr. said. "The first was that I was happy because I would finally have my chance. The second was that it was sad that the family was being broken up. But we had never been together much, anyway."

Last year the three Alomars did get together for one game—Sandy Jr. and Roberto as players and Sandy as a coach. The Alomars are baseball's All-Star family.

THE DAVISES: GLENN FINDS HIS PURPOSE IN LIFE

Glenn Davis had a terrible childhood. His father, a minor-league baseball player, and mother divorced while he was young. Glenn took it pretty hard. He responded by getting into a lot of trouble.

"I was your basic juvenile delinquent," Glenn said. "I was living in hell. I would ask God why this was all happening to me."

Glenn's mother worked long hours. He never saw his father after the divorce. "I felt alone," he said. "I didn't think anyone loved me. I didn't know what my purpose in life was. I remember asking myself, *Why was I ever born into this world? Who am I? What am I?*"

Glenn Davis gets ready on first base.

Glenn Finds Baseball

By the time he had reached the seventh grade, Glenn began to discover that his purpose in life was sports.

"I just always had the knack for swinging the bat," he said. "From the time I was 7 till I was 17, I was always the best."

Glenn and his mother fought often. She was very strict and didn't like the idea of his playing baseball. She didn't want him to follow in his father's footsteps. But Glenn was determined—baseball was the one thing that he did well.

Glenn attended the University High School in Jacksonville, Florida. The school's baseball coach was George Davis. Davis's son, also named George but nicknamed Storm, was a high school baseball player, too. George took an interest in Glenn when he saw his potential.

One day he said to Glenn, "You know, the way you hit the ball, you could make a living at this game someday."

The Davis Duo

Suddenly Glenn had a purpose in life. He stopped getting into trouble and began concentrating on baseball. He and Storm both showed major-league potential in high school. Storm didn't hit as well as Glenn, but he had a big-league pitching arm. Together they formed a powerful combination. Glenn remembers:

"In high school they called us the Davis Duo," said Glenn. "We won two state titles and were runners-up the other year."

After graduating from high school, Glenn moved in with Coach Davis's family. Glenn called George and Norma Davis Mom and Dad. He became a part of the family as their foster son.

Norma Davis is a Christian radio talk-show host. She and Glenn grew very close and Glenn began to take religion seriously. To this day, he remains a devout Christian.

"Now I don't just say I'm a devout Christian," he said. "I walk it, talk it, and breathe it."

Glenn and Storm in the Majors

After they graduated from high school, Storm and Glenn were both drafted by the Baltimore Orioles. Storm joined the Orioles, but Glenn decided to go to college. After a year of hitting home runs for the University of Georgia, Glenn was drafted again—now by the Houston Astros. This time Glenn decided to join the pros.

Storm reached the major leagues in 1982. Glenn reached the majors two years later. Storm, who was only 20 years old, had an excellent rookie year. He won eight games and lost only four, with a solid 3.49 ERA. In 1983, Storm moved into the Baltimore starting rotation. He won 13 games in helping the Orioles to the AL pennant.

Storm pitched very well in the play-offs, shutting out the White Sox for six innings. Then, in the World Series, he beat the Phillies in the fourth game and gave Baltimore a 3-1 lead. Baltimore won the World Series in the next game. At age 21, Storm had become a World Series hero.

Although he hasn't had a chance to play in the World Series, Glenn Davis has made his presence known in the major leagues. Playing in the Houston Astrodome, where home runs are very hard to hit, Glenn has slugged 20 or more home runs for 6 straight seasons. In 1986, he was runner-up to Mike Schmidt in the balloting for the MVP award. The Astros won the NL Western Division championship that year for only the second time in their history.

Storm Davis unleashes a pitch.

Mitchell B. Reibel/Sportschrome

In 1987, Storm was traded to the San Diego Padres, who then shipped him to the Oakland A's. There he was a member of two AL pennant winners and won another World Series ring. The next year he signed a multi-million-dollar contract with the Kansas City Royals.

Before the 1991 season, Glenn was traded to Storm's old team, the Baltimore Orioles. Baltimore's Memorial Stadium is a much easier place for hitting home runs than is the Astrodome. Bob Watson, Glenn's former batting coach, commented: "I'd be very, very surprised if he doesn't hit 35 to 45 home runs there, and it definitely wouldn't surprise me if he hit 50." Baltimore former manager Frank Robinson added: "When I got called about the trade, I just sat there thinking, *We got Glenn Davis!* I couldn't sleep at night, I was so excited."

Glenn is happy to be playing for Baltimore, but he is just as excited with the work he does for orphans. He has helped sponsor and build a home for boys.

"I want to provide a positive identity for them," he said. "These kids are going to be so proud of me. They can say, 'My dad's a professional baseball player.'"

After a difficult beginning, Glenn Davis has found the answer to his childhood questions. Together, he and his foster brother, Storm, represent what being a professional is all about.

THE PERRYS: OUT OF THE FRIDGE'S SHADOW

Michael Dean Perry is a huge man, standing 6 feet tall and weighing 280 pounds. But in his family, he's the little brother in more ways than one. His elder brother William, nicknamed "the Refrigerator" ("the Fridge," for short), is 6 feet 2 inches tall and has weighed as much as 365 pounds! Now the Fridge has lost weight and weighs "only" 325 pounds. Still, between Michael Dean and William, that makes 605 pounds in the NFL.

The "Refrigerator" checks out the action from the sidelines.

"The Fridge"

William was the tenth child and Michael Dean the twelfth and last child born to Hollie and Inez Perry. They grew up in Aiken, South Carolina. Even as a child William was huge. He weighed over 13 pounds at birth, and by the time he reached the first grade, he was 50 pounds heavier than any other student. As a young boy, William was a bit of a bully, but his mother soon put an end to that.

"I used to beat people up because I was bigger than anyone else," he said. "But whenever I did it, my momma would whip me good."

By the time William entered ninth grade at Aiken High School, he had grown to his present height and weighed 285 pounds. He became a South Carolina legend in high school. Many colleges wanted "the Refrigerator," as he was now known. But William decided to attend nearby Clemson University, playing defensive tackle. He set a Clemson University career record by sacking opposing quarterbacks 27 times. In 1984, he was named an All-American at defensive tackle.

William's size made him a controversial choice when the Chicago Bears selected him in the 1985 draft. Experts felt he weighed far too much to have the speed needed to play in the pros. Defensive coach Buddy Ryan described drafting Perry as a "wasted pick."

William proved the experts wrong, though. Showing incredible agility for a man his size, he earned a starting position as defensive tackle. "The Refrigerator" was a huge hit with the Chicago fans. He seemed like a great, big teddy bear come to life. The Bears kept winning games, and "the Fridge" kept making headlines.

Then, during a Monday Night Football game, William became a national hero. In the third quarter, the Bears had the ball on the 1-yard line. Head coach Mike Ditka broke with tradition and put "the Fridge" in at fullback. William got the handoff during the next play and plowed into the end zone. Touchdown!

Overnight, William Perry became a household word. TV talk shows wanted him as a guest. Companies wanted him to do commercials for their products. The Bears made a hit record and video called "The Super

Bowl Shuffle" that featured "the Fridge" prominently. To cap it all off, he scored another touchdown in the Super Bowl at the end of the season, helping the Bears beat the Patriots 46-10. It was an incredible season.

Still, William didn't let the attention get to him. "All of this stuff is something that kind of happened overnight," he said. "It's just fun to me. Sure, I'm glad I got the chance to be on TV. I thank the good Lord for letting it all happen, but I let things come and I let things go. I know this is all going to end someday."

Michael Dean: All-Pro

Michael was also very large as a youngster, but in his household, this was nothing out of the ordinary. All his brothers were big. They all loved their baby brother. To this day, Micheal Dean thinks of his brothers as his heroes in life.

"I really didn't have a public figure I looked up to," he said. "I patterned myself after my brothers. They were exceptional athletes."

Michael Dean was quietly making a name for himself. Following in William's footsteps, he too was an All-American defensive tackle at Clemson. He also broke his brother's quarterback sack record. In 1988, he was drafted by the Cleveland Browns. He listened to his big brother's advice on life in the pros: "Take it in stride," William told Michael Dean. "Whatever happens, happens."

As it turned out, good things happened for Michael

Michael Dean Perry—the Cleveland Browns' top "dawg."

Dean. He made All-Pro in both 1989 and 1990, and was one of the most important members of the Dawg Pound— the nickname of Cleveland's crunching defense.

"The Dawg Pound is dangerous," said Michael Dean. "You have fans out there venting their frustrations. They're cheering and hollering. The fans elevate us all to top form."

While Michael Dean was making All-Pro, William was having problems in Chicago. He kept putting on too much weight. Coach Ditka was publicly critical of his performance. Now it was time for William to listen to Michael Dean's advice.

"By the mere fact that the Bears were winning in 1985," said Michael, "nobody made a big deal about William's weight. But now that the Bears aren't doing so well, you have to point the finger somewhere. He's almost at the point he's burned out."

"He's a phenomenal athlete," Michael Dean reminded fans. "He deserves the recognition."

"The Fridge" came back and had an excellent 1990 season, as the Bears won the Central Division. "The Fridge" is only 28, and Michael is only 26. The NFL hasn't seen the end of the Perry brothers.

Barry Bonds learned from his dad how to deal with the pressures of being in the major leagues. Brett Hull learned not to imitate his father's style of play, but to create his own. Reggie and Cheryl Miller learned about competition in their backyard one-on-one games. By helping, sharing, and learning from one another, the families in this book were able to reach outstanding heights—in sports and in life.